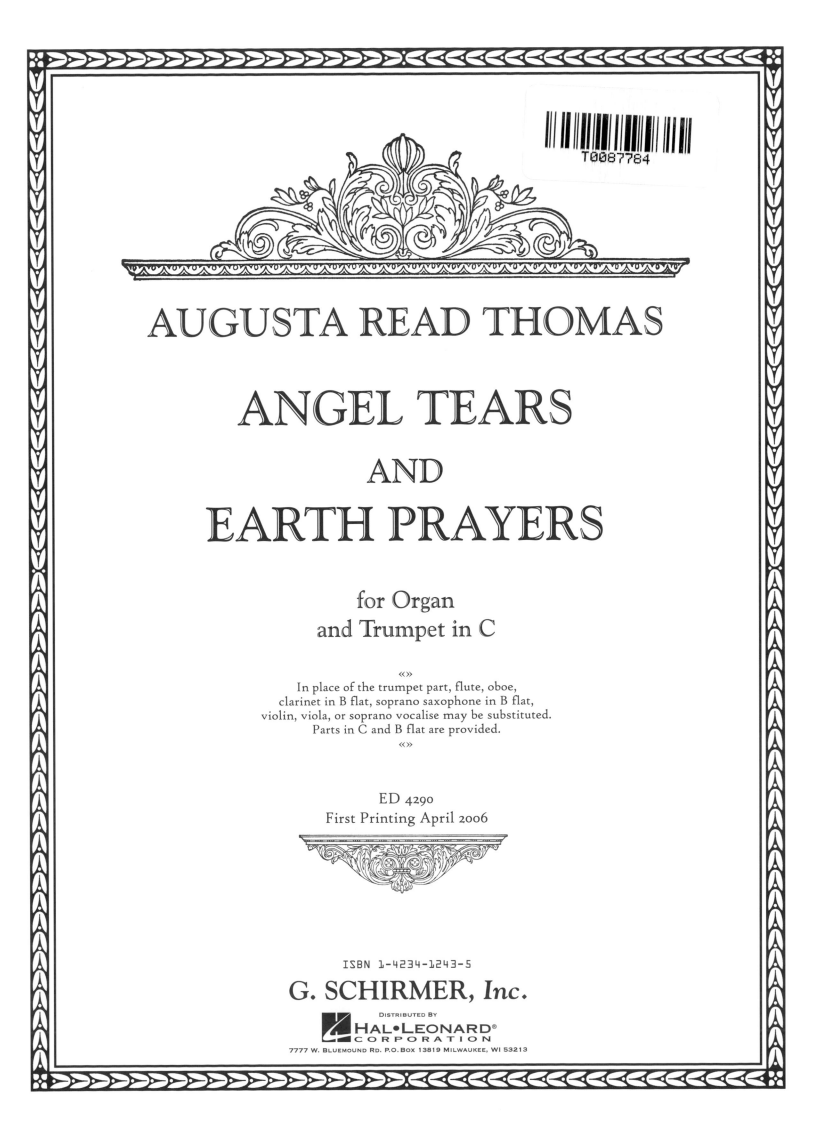

AUGUSTA READ THOMAS

ANGEL TEARS

AND

EARTH PRAYERS

for Organ
and Trumpet in C

«»
In place of the trumpet part, flute, oboe,
clarinet in B flat, soprano saxophone in B flat,
violin, viola, or soprano vocalise may be substituted.
Parts in C and B flat are provided.
«»

ED 4290
First Printing April 2006

ISBN 1-4234-1243-5

G. SCHIRMER, Inc.

DISTRIBUTED BY
HAL•LEONARD®
CORPORATION
7777 W. BLUEMOUND RD. P.O. BOX 13819 MILWAUKEE, WI 53213

This work was commissioned by the American Guild of Organists
and was given its first performance during their annual conference
on 3 July 2006, Valparaiso University Chapel of the Resurrection
Valparaiso, Indiana.

This work was composed with the idea that it might be used in all kinds of liturgical settings.
The two movements may be performed separately or together.
In place of the trumpet part, flute, oboe, clarinet in B flat, soprano saxophone in B flat,
violin, viola, or soprano vocalise may be substituted. Parts in C and B flat are provided.

The composer would like to thank John Sherer for his invaluable help.

Duration ca. 5 minutes.

in memory of Jock Elliott

ANGEL TEARS AND EARTH PRAYERS
(for Organ and Trumpet)

Registration by John Sherer

Augusta Read Thomas
(2006)

Angel Tears

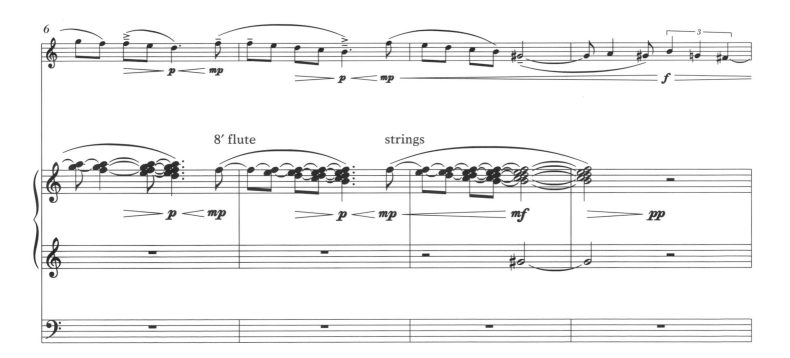

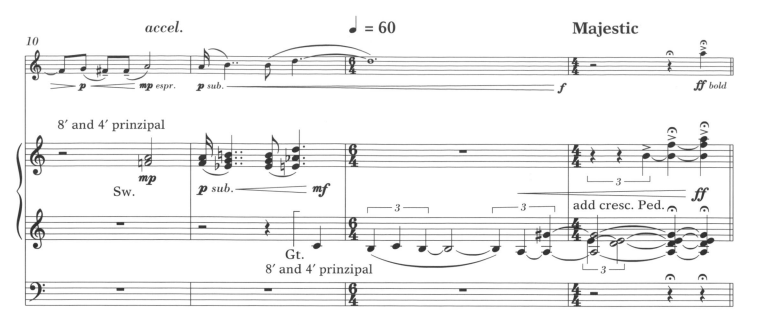

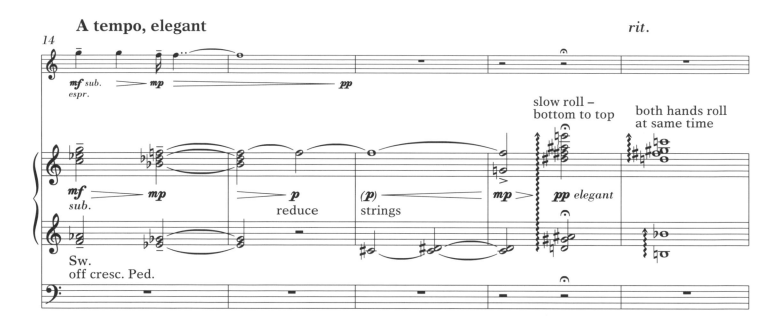

AUGUSTA READ THOMAS

ANGEL TEARS

AND

EARTH PRAYERS

solo part in C

ED 4290
First Printing April 2006

G. SCHIRMER, Inc.

ISBN 1-4234-1243-5

DISTRIBUTED BY
HAL•LEONARD®
CORPORATION
7777 W. BLUEMOUND RD. P.O. BOX 13819 MILWAUKEE, WI 53213

C Instruments

in memory of Jock Elliott

ANGEL TEARS AND EARTH PRAYERS
(for Organ and Trumpet)

Registration by John Sherer

Augusta Read Thomas

Angel Tears

Earth Prayers

AUGUSTA READ THOMAS

ANGEL TEARS
AND
EARTH PRAYERS

solo part in B flat

ED 4290
First Printing April 2006

ISBN 1-4234-1243-5

G. SCHIRMER, Inc.

DISTRIBUTED BY

HAL•LEONARD®
CORPORATION

7777 W. BLUEMOUND RD. P.O. BOX 13819 MILWAUKEE, WI 53213

Bb Instruments

in memory of Jock Elliott

ANGEL TEARS AND EARTH PRAYERS
(for Organ and Trumpet)

Registration by John Sherer

Augusta Read Thomas

Angel Tears

Earth Prayers

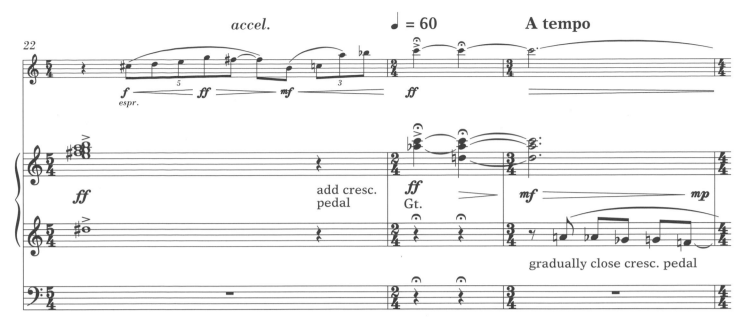

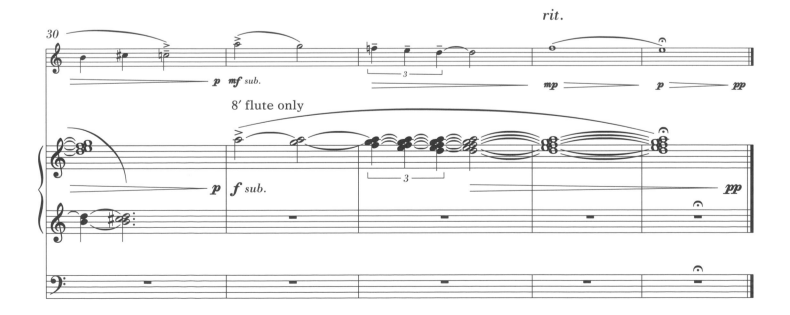

Earth Prayers